This book belongs to

_____

This book is dedicated to my children - Mikey, Kobe, and Jojo.

Copyright © 2023 Grow Grit Press LLC. All rights reserved. No part of this book may be reproduced in any form without permission in writing from the publisher. Please send bulk order requests to info@ninjalifehacks.tv

Paperback ISBN: 978-1-63731-805-8
Hardcover ISBN: 978-1-63731-807-2
eBook ISBN: 978-1-63731-806-5

Printed and bound in the USA.
NinjaLifeHacks.tv

by Mary Nhin

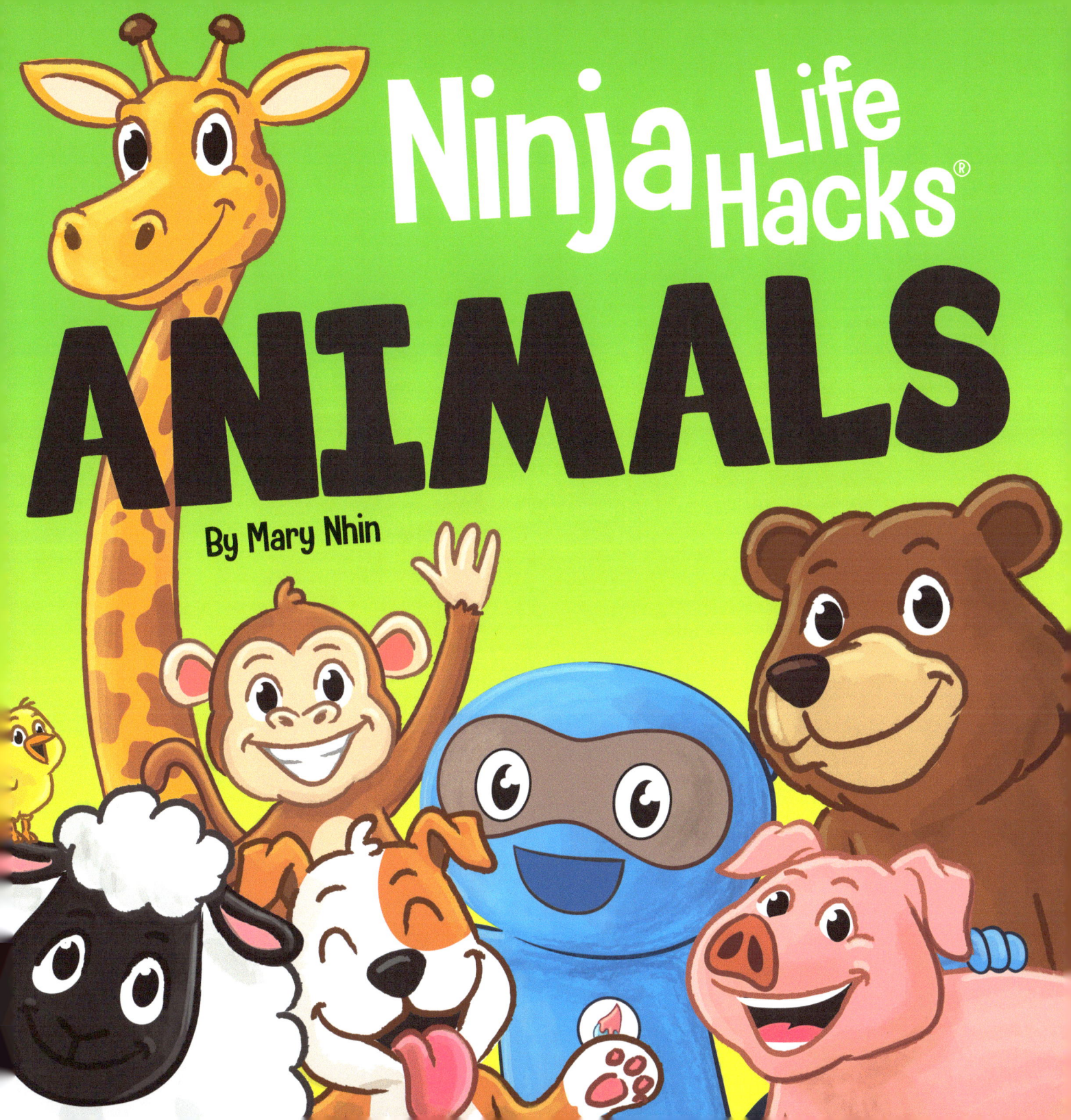

Ninjas know their animals,
And that they have feelings too,

That's why ninjas are patient with them,
No matter what the animals do.

Respectful Ninja loves the farm **dog**
As she helps herd the **sheep**.
Lazy Ninja prefers to hide in the barn,
Behind a bale of hay to sleep!

Caring Ninja looks on and
Appreciates the mother and her **ducklings**' bond.

Patient Ninja feeds the **chickens**,
As they peck around outside of the coop.

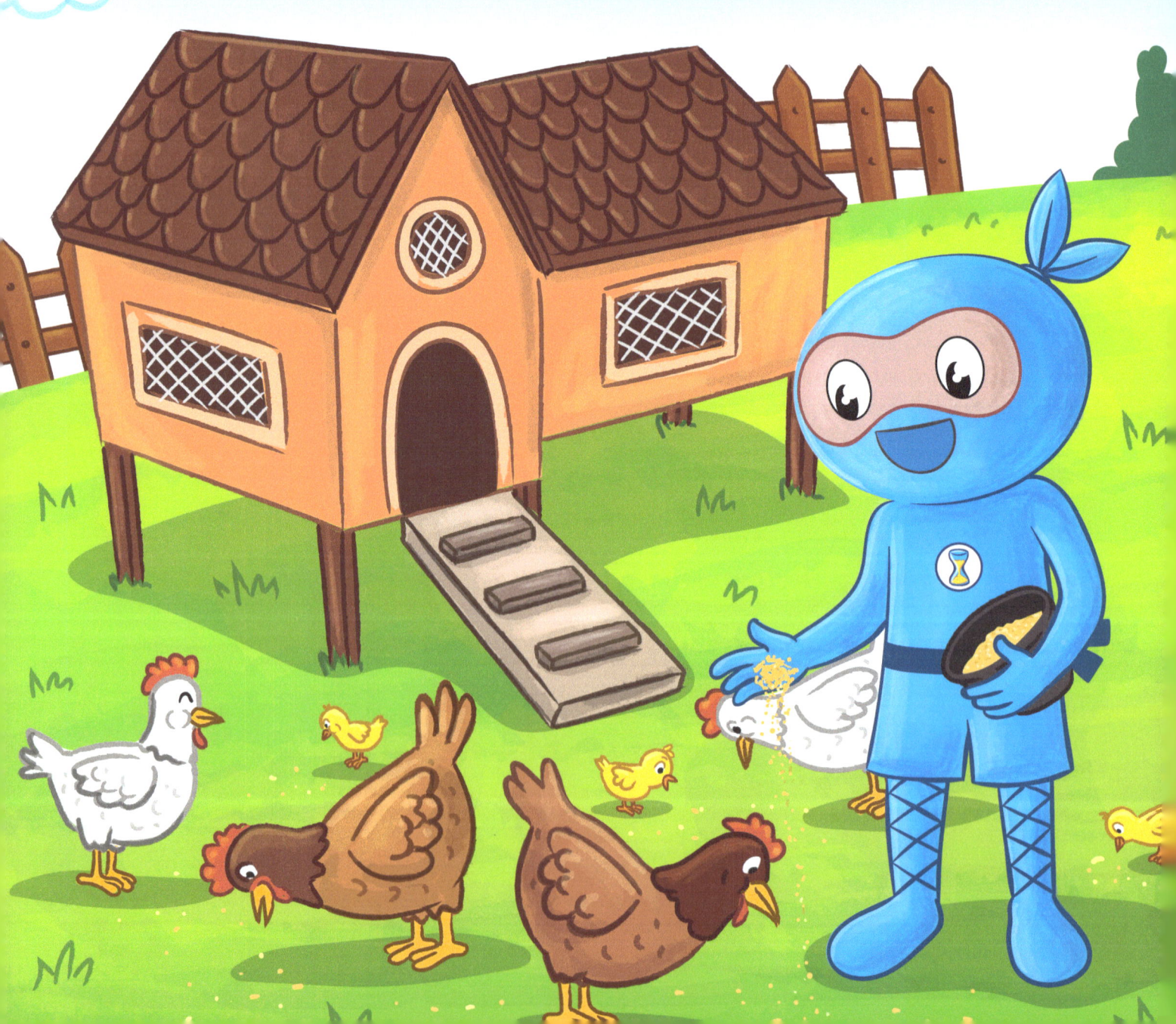

Ambitious Ninja gives the **pigs** a bath,
While Hopeful Ninja hopes they will stay clean.
Shy Ninja sits on the porch, petting the **cat**,
Watching the entire farm scene.

Other ninjas prefer animals of the jungle,
Like **Lions**, **tigers**, and **bears**.
Unplugged Ninja loves to explore the rainforest,
While Curious Ninja blows bubbles in the air.

Impulsive Ninja reaches out to pet the **panda**,
While Perfect Ninja marvels at the tall trees.
Compassionate Ninja cuddles a baby **monkey**,
While Brave Ninja swings from the vines. **WHEE!**

Ninjas know all sorts of animals,
From **very large** to **super small**.

But of all the ninjas that like the animals,
Love Ninja **loves** them all!

Continue the learning with our fun lesson plans which include superpower skills practice, STEM activity, craft, and more! Visit ninjalifehacks.tv

 @marynhin @officialninjalifehacks
#NinjaLifeHacks

 Ninja Life Hacks

 Mary Nhin   Ninja Life Hacks

 @officialninjalifehacks